TOTEM POLE

Text copyright © 1990 by Diane Hoyt-Goldsmith.
Photographs copyright © 1990 by Lawrence Migdale.
Text illustrations copyright © 1990 by David Boxley.
All rights reserved. Published by Scholastic Inc., 730 Broadway,
New York, NY 10003, by arrangement with Holiday House, Inc.
Printed in the U.S.A.
ISBN 0-590-46459-0

1 2 3 4 5 6 7 8 9 10   09   99 98 97 96 95 94 93 92

ACKNOWLEDGMENTS

In creating this book, we enjoyed the enthusiasm and cooperation of many people. We would like to express our special appreciation to David and Liz Boxley, and their sons David and Zachary, for sharing the experience of carving and raising the totem pole with us; to Shirley and Sherwood Duryea, for their on-site support and encouragement; and to Gerald "Jake" Jones, Tribal Chairman of the Klallam and the people of the Port Gamble Reservation for creating the opportunity for this story and for their generous hospitality.

For more information about the carver and his work, you may write to:
    David Boxley
    P.O. Box 527
    Kingston, WA 98346

TOTEM POLE

BY DIANE HOYT-GOLDSMITH

PHOTOGRAPHS BY LAWRENCE MIGDALE

SCHOLASTIC INC.
New York Toronto London Auckland Sydney

*This book is dedicated to
David's great-grandfather,
Albert Bolton,
of Metlakatla, Alaska.*

*He was born in 1894
when the old ways were still new.
His memories of the Tsimshian traditions
are a precious heritage.*

David, in the woods near his home, wears a Tsimshian robe and headdress. The headdress has a frontlet carved in the shape of an eagle and is decorated with ermine skins.

 My name is David. I live in a small town called Kingston in Washington State. In the summer, I like to hunt for salmonberries and blackberries in the fields near our house.

My brother and I like to look out over Puget Sound, watching for the ferry from Seattle. Sometimes, we spot a pair of eagles flying high overhead. This makes us feel lucky because our family belongs to the Eagle Clan, which is our family group within the Tsimshian *(TSIM-shee-an)* tribe.

Our father is an Indian. He was brought up by his grandparents in Metlakatla *(MET-lah-CAT-lah)*, on Annette Island in Alaska. He was raised in the old ways and traditions. He learned how to hunt, to fish, and to carve.

In our tribe, a person belongs to the same clan as his mother does. Our mother is not Indian. Her ancestors emigrated to the United States from Europe many generations ago. When I was two years old, she was adopted in a special ceremony by two members of the Eagle Clan in Metlakatla. This makes my brother and me members of the Eagle Clan too.

My father is an artist, a wood-carver. Ever since I was little, I have watched him take a piece of wood and carve a creature from it. Sometimes it is a wolf, sometimes a bear, and sometimes an eagle, the symbol and totem of our clan.

David and his brother watch the ferry from Edmonds, a suburb of Seattle, as it comes into Kingston harbor.

In the workshop, David's father shows him a wolf mask he is carving. The jaws can open and close. On the workbench, there is a row of handmade knives used to carve fine details in the wood.

The finished mask is called Wolf's Den. *The wolf mask has been mounted on a painted and carved panel. When the jaws open, a tiny spirit peers out.*

Using many different tools, my father cuts into the wood where the figure he is carving lies hidden. As he works, he tells me that he is uncovering the spirit which is hidden in the wood. He says it is a spirit only he can see.

In the early days, the Tsimshian people made many things out of wood. Each object they carved was useful and beautiful. They made their own bowls and storage boxes. They made hooks for fishing and weapons for hunting. They carved masks and made clothing. They made their own canoes, their own homes, and they made totem poles to record their legends and to honor important people.

David's father shows him how a halibut swims up to take the hook. The Tsimshian carve different hooks for different fish. A large hook can catch a large fish and a small hook can catch a small fish.

On the top of the hook there is a Spirit Helper carved in the shape of a halibut. The Spirit Helper does two things: the first is to attract the fish to the hook and the second is to show ownership. The person who owns the hook carves his own family crest as the Spirit Helper.

Once my father made a halibut hook carved from two pieces of yellow cedar. He explained how the Tsimshian would use it to catch fish. The hook is shaped like a fish and has a very sharp piece of bone inside it. There is a Spirit Helper carved on the top to attract the halibut.

The baited hook is lowered into the water by using a long piece of cedar bark which has been twisted into a rope. Because of the way it has been carved, the hook moves like a weak or injured fish as it floats underwater. The halibut, swimming nearby, is attracted by the motion and sucks the hook into his mouth to get the bait. When the fish opens his mouth to spit the hook out, he gets caught on the sharp bone.

Today we can go to a market to buy fish to cook for dinner. But my father still carves the halibut hook because he wants me to know how it was in the old days. He wants me to know all the Tsimshian traditions.

My father has a special cedar box. It is very important to him because it was made by my great-great-grandfather five generations ago. My father painted an eagle on the lid, and now he keeps his carving tools inside.

The box was first used to store food. When my father was a young boy, he was in charge of keeping the food box safe. When his family went out to hunt or fish, he carried the box from the boat up to the camp and stored it in a safe place. The foods his family had prepared for the journey were kept inside the box—the dried meat and fish, and the hardtack. These were the only foods the family would have to eat while they were camping.

My father says that even now, when he opens the box to take out a tool, he can smell the foods that were once stored inside. The faint scent brings him strong memories of the salt air, the hardtack, the fresh salmon, and even the smoke of the cooking fire where his family gathered. These memories are precious to him. The smells make the past come alive, he says.

When I open the box, all I can smell are the steel and leather tools inside. But the past comes alive for me when I hear the strike of the adze and hear my father tell his stories. He likes to tell me what it was like to grow up in Alaska.

One of my favorite stories is a Tsimshian tale called "The Legend of the Eagle and the Young Chief." Maybe I like it best because I belong to the Eagle Clan.

This box was made by David's great-great-grandfather as a storage box for food. Now David's father uses it as a toolbox. The adzes in front are made from the elbows of alder or yew tree branches.

The Legend of the Eagle and the Young Chief
A Tsimshian Tale

Once, in days of old, a young Tsimshian chief was walking on a beach near his village. He was thinking of the successful fishing trip he had that morning.

Suddenly, the silence of the shoreline was interrupted by a loud noise in the woods nearby. When the chief got closer, he saw that a magnificent eagle was trapped by a piece of old fishnet. The eagle's feathers were tangled in the brush and his eyes were sad.

The young chief knelt down and began to free the great bird. Very carefully, he loosened the knots of the net and gently cleared away the brambles. Suddenly, the bird flew up to freedom.

In those days, there was a spirit in everything: in animals, in trees, even in the rocks along the shoreline. The chief, when he performed his kind act, did not know that this eagle was special. He came from the world of spirits.

Later that year, times were hard for the young chief's village. Food was scarce and many people began to go hungry. The young chief was very worried, because he didn't want his people to starve.

One day, the chief was walking along the beach, wondering what he should do. Suddenly, a beautiful salmon dropped at his feet in the sand, alive, its silver sides flashing. When the chief looked up, he saw Eagle gliding away into the distance.

For many days thereafter, Eagle brought fish and left them on the beach for the villagers. Then, Eagle began to bring seals. As time went on, he brought larger and larger animals to feed the people of the village. Eventually, he even delivered a whale onto the beach.

The eagle was a spirit, and nothing was too difficult for him to do. Because he brought food to the people of the village, the villagers passed safely through the time of famine and rejoiced in days of plenty.

All this was done because the young chief had once saved Eagle's life. When the chief acted kindly, the eagle later paid him back with kindness, but magnified a thousand times.

10

When my father first began to teach me about the Tsimshian songs, dances, and legends, he made some special clothes for me to wear. These clothes are called "regalia." They are worn for certain ceremonies, dances, and celebrations.

Sometimes in the afternoons, I go to my father's workshop. I look inside the trunk that holds all the regalia he has made. I dress in my special clothes to practice the dances my father taught me.

The first thing my father made for me is a headdress out of leather and decorated with ermine skins. On the front, there is a small eagle's face carved from a piece of cedar wood and painted blue and brown. This is called a frontlet. The eagle is shown on all our regalia because the eagle is our family crest. My Indian name is Lap'aigh laskeeg *(lah-pah-AG-a-lah-SKEEK)*. It means "He Who Flies Like the Eagle" in the Tsimshian language.

In the tradition of our people, a name is something you can inherit from another family member or you can earn a name by performing a special good deed. My father has four Tsimshian names. The two most important names translate as "The First to Potlatch" and "He Who Works with the Cedar." My little brother has a name, too. It means "He Who Slides Like a Halibut." He earned that name because of the funny way he slid across the floor when he was a baby learning to crawl.

My father made me an apron out of deerskin which is painted with an eagle design. I have leggings made of soft leather. They have a fringe with deer hooves hanging down. The hooves knock together as I dance and make a rattling sound as I move.

I also have a button blanket that I wear. On the back there is another large eagle design. It is outlined in hundreds of tiny white buttons. In the old days, the Tsimshian blankets were first woven from cedar bark and then decorated with rows of tiny white shells. But in the 1800s, when Europeans began to trade with the tribes along the coast, the Indians began to use bright red "trade cloth" for the blankets and machine-made buttons of mother-of-pearl for decoration.

The eagle design on the back of David's button blanket is made by sewing hundreds of tiny mother-of-pearl buttons into a pattern.

12

David finds a new treasure inside the chest in his father's workshop. This knife is used in a Tsimshian dance and has an eagle's head carved on top.

13

CARVING THE POLE

My father is carving a totem pole for the Klallam *(KLAH-lum)* Indians who live on the Port Gamble Reservation near our home. Although my father belongs to a different tribe, the Tsimshian, he was asked to carve the pole because of his skill. It is common among the Northwest Coast Indians for one tribe to invite an artist from another tribe to carve a pole for them. The pole will be made from a single log, forty feet long. It will have animals and figures carved on it, important characters from Klallam myths and legends.

My father says that a totem pole is like a signboard. He tells me that it is a system for passing on legends and stories from one generation to another for people who have no written language. A totem pole is like a library for a tribe!

The first step in making a totem pole is to find a straight tree. It must be wide enough to make a strong pole. The best trees for a totem pole have few branches. Where a branch joins the trunk a knot forms, making the carving very difficult.

Nearly all totem poles are carved from cedar logs. Cedar trees grow very straight and are common in the evergreen forests along the coastline near our home. The wood of the cedar is soft and easy to carve. It does not rot and insects will not destroy it. A totem pole carved from a cedar log can last a hundred years or more.

After the right tree is found and cut down, all the branches are removed with an axe and the bark is stripped from the outside of the log. In the old days, the Indians had no saws or axes, so even cutting the tree down was a harder job than it is today. Back then, the carvers used a hammer and chisel to cut a wedge at the base of the tree. This weakened the tree, and in a strong wind storm, the tree would fall.

David and his father look for a tall, straight tree in the woods near their home.

When the log is ready to be carved, my father makes a drawing of how the pole will look when it is finished. He draws the animals for the totem pole on a sheet of paper. He might begin by drawing each animal separately, but before he starts to carve he will draw a picture of how the completed pole will look.

Next he uses a stick of charcoal to make a drawing on the log itself. Then he stands up on the log to see how the figures and animals look. When he is satisfied with the drawing, he takes up his tools and begins to carve.

David's father carves a totem pole on the Klallam Reservation in Little Boston. He works from a drawing which he transfers onto the log. The charcoal outline of the Bear's eyebrows are visible on the wood.

A sign posted at the entrance to the Klallam Reservation says that brush picking, woodcutting, clam digging, crabbing, fishing, and hunting can be done only by members of the tribe. Because nature is important to the Klallam way of life, it must be protected.

15

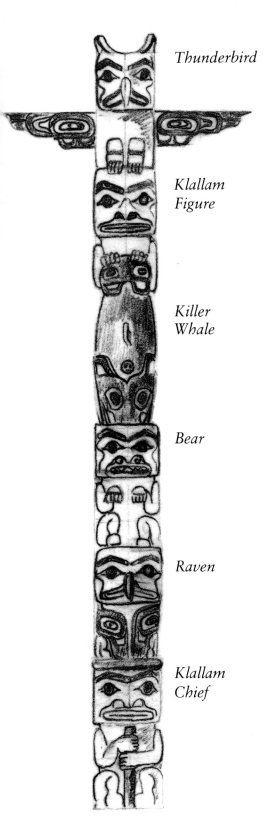

Thunderbird

Klallam Figure

Killer Whale

Bear

Raven

Klallam Chief

The totem pole for the Klallam tribe has six figures, one on top of the other. At the very top of the pole is the Thunderbird. He brings good luck to the Klallam village. The Klallam people believe the Thunderbird lives on the Olympic mountain range, across the water from their reservation, in the place where the mountains touch the sky. They say that when Thunderbird catches the great Killer Whale, you can hear thunder and see lightning in the sky.

Below Thunderbird is the figure who represents the Klallam people. The figure holds Killer Whale by the tail. Together, they tell the legend of a tribal member named Charlie who rode out to sea on the back of a Killer Whale.

The fourth animal on the pole is Bear, who provided the Indian people with many important things. His fur gave warmth and clothing. His meat gave food. His claws and teeth were used for trinkets and charms and to decorate clothing.

The next figure is Raven, who brought light to the Indian people by stealing the Sun from Darkness. Raven is the great trickster. Sometimes he does things that are good, but sometimes he does things that are bad.

The last figure on the pole is a Klallam Chief. The chief on the pole holds a "speaker stick," a symbol of his leadership and his important position in the tribe. In the Klallam culture, when a chief holds the speaker stick, all the people pay attention and listen to what he says.

As my father carves the pole, he brings all of these characters to life. He works on the pole every day. He uses many tools: the adze, chisels, and handmade knives. He even uses a chain saw for the largest cuts!

This totem pole is special to me. I am finally old enough to help my father with the work. He lets me sweep away the wood shavings as he carves. I can also take care of the tools he uses—the adze, the saws, the handmade knives, and the chisels.

As I get older, I'll learn how to use my father's carving tools safely and to help him really carve a pole. But for now, I just practice on some bits of wood I find lying around. Like my father, I look for the animal shapes hidden inside the wood.

16

David and his father walk along the pole to check the progress of the carving. Kneeling on top, David learns to judge whether the figures on the pole are lined up correctly.

17

Using a handmade knife, David's father carves fine details into the pole.

Striking the wood with the adze makes a unique pattern on the pole. This pattern differs with every carver and is like a signature of the artist who carves the pole.

In the old days, it used to take a year to carve a totem pole. In those days, the blade of the adze was made of stone and wasn't nearly as sharp as the steel blades my father uses today. Knives, for the carving of fine details, were made from beaver teeth or from large shells.

My father says that it is the artist's skill with the adze that makes a totem pole great. Each artist has his own way of carving. The strokes of the adze create a pattern in the wood, like small ripples across the wide water.

In the old days, carvers had special songs to chant while they worked. The chanting helped them keep up a rhythm with their adzing strokes. Now my father likes to work to songs on the radio. He works to the beat of rock 'n' roll.

My father makes the work look easy. He cuts into the wood quickly, as if it were as soft as soap. I know carving is much harder than he makes it look. I know because I've tried it.

18

David paints the eye shape of the Klallam Figure black.

After all the figures and animals are carved into the log, I help my father paint the pole. We make the eyes dark. We paint the mouths red. Whale's back and dorsal fin are black. Raven and Thunderbird have wings with patterns of red and black. The colors my father shows me are taken from the old traditions of the Tsimshian people. From a distance, the pole will look powerful and strong.

Finally, after two months of hard work, my father puts away his tools and packs up his paintbrushes. The totem pole is finished.

RAISING THE POLE

David's mother helps her sons dress for the pole-raising ceremony.

The Klallam tribe decides to hold a special ceremony to raise the totem pole. It will follow the ancient traditions of the Northwest Coast Indian people. After the ceremony, there will be a feast like the potlatch of the old days. There will be many guests. There will be traditional songs and dances, and food prepared by the villagers. If this were a traditional potlatch, the Klallam would give money or gifts to every guest.

On the day of the ceremony, we arrive on the Klallam Reservation early. I look at the pole, lying on its back in the early morning light. Each figure on the pole is strong and seems to have a spirit all its own. Looking at the totem pole, I can hardly believe my father made it.

Soon the guests begin to arrive. Many are from the Klallam village. Others are from Seattle and the surrounding towns. Some people have even come from other states.

My father and I dress in our regalia. Although my little brother is too young to dance, he wears his button blanket and headdress for the occasion. Most of my family have come to celebrate the raising of the pole. My mother is here with my grandmother and grandfather. I know my father wishes that *his* grandfather could be here too. Although my great-grandfather is in Alaska, we know he is thinking about us today.

Moving very slowly, the villagers and guests carry the totem pole down the road to the place where it will be raised.

When all the guests have arrived, my father invites everyone to help carry the pole to the place where it will be raised. It weighs over three thousand pounds and it takes fifty strong men and women to carry it. Long pieces of wood are placed underneath the back of the pole. Standing two by two, the people lift the pole when my father gives the command. They carry it slowly down the road to the place where it will stand.

In the old days, every totem pole stood so it faced the water. This was because the visitors to a village would always arrive by canoe. But today, things are different. Since people come to the reservation by car, the pole is placed to face the road.

It used to be that a totem pole was raised in position by hand, with many people pulling it up with ropes. The modern way is to use a powerful truck with a crane attached. The crane slowly lifts the pole while a group of singers chant and dance.

To prepare the pole for raising, people remove the carrying boards. David's father circles the pole for a final check to make sure the pole is ready. A hole six feet deep has been prepared for the base of the pole.

As the pole is raised higher and higher, their voices grow louder and louder. It takes a number of tries to get the pole in the right position, but finally it is done. The pole stands straight, facing south toward the road that leads into the Klallam Reservation.

A group of native dancers play their drums and chant as the pole is slowly raised into position. They wear button blankets decorated with their family crests.

When the pole is nearly straight, David's father uses a hook to steady the pole before cement is poured in the hole.

Now it is time for my father and me to dance. Holding ceremonial wooden adzes, we begin to perform the Carver's Dance at the base of the totem pole. This dance was created by my father to show that the work on the pole is finished. We dance to show how proud we are.

Our movements tell about our search through the forest for a strong, straight tree. We pretend to cut the tree down and carve designs into the log with our ceremonial adzes. Then we put our tools aside, and pick up a fan of white eagle feathers, one in each hand. We swoop in circles, doing an eagle dance to celebrate our eagle crest and show the symbol of our clan to all the people watching.

David and his father perform the Carver's Dance at the base of the pole.

After the pole raising and dances, the guests are invited to a traditional feast. The Klallam tribesmen grill salmon from Puget Sound over charcoal, or thread the fish on wooden stakes made of cedar to broil over the hot coals. Fresh cockles and clams are steamed in wet burlap over heated stones. There are lots of other good things to eat: Indian fry bread with jam or maple syrup, corn on the cob, potato salad, and homemade berry pies.

A member of the Klallam tribe barbecues salmon over the coals. In front, the salmon is threaded on cedar stakes to cook in the traditional manner.

Dressed in full regalia, David performs the Salmon Dance. The white feathers in his headdress show that he is a member of the Eagle Clan.

When the feast is over, my father and I dance once again. We perform the Salmon Dance that describes the hunt for salmon, our most important source of food. We act out the casting of nets over the water, the circling of boats to close in on the schools of fish, the salmon jumping out of the water, jumping and jumping again. When the salmon jump, my father and I shout "Ai-yoo *(eye-YOH)*!" which means "There the fish jump!" The crowd, watching us dance, shouts "Gikwah *(geek-WAH)*!" This is Tsimshian for "Do it again!" Each time a fish breaks from the water in a leap for freedom, the crowd shouts "Gikwah! Gikwah!"

27

Late in the day, the cement around the base of the pole is still wet. The totem pole is held in place by strong ropes tied to trees on every side. Tomorrow the ropes will be removed.

28

 As I listen to the chanted songs and move to the ancient music of my ancestors, I am proud. I am proud to have a father who can transform a straight cedar log into a magnificent totem pole. In the forest, it was a beautiful tree. Then my father saw in it the shapes of Thunderbird, the Klallam figure, Raven, Whale, Bear, and the Klallam Chief. He brought them all to life with his skill. I am proud of my people. I am proud to be the son of a Tsimshian carver.

The completed totem pole stands in Little Boston to greet travelers who journey to the Klallam Reservation. The figures on the pole are Thunderbird at the top, then a Klallam Figure holding Killer Whale by the tail, then Bear, Raven, and the Klallam Chief with his speaker stick.

GLOSSARY

Adze: A tool shaped like an axe. It is used by the Tsimshian to create a pattern on the surface of a wood carving. The adze handle is handmade from the elbow of a yew or alder branch. The blade is made of steel.

Ai-yoo: *(eye-YOH)* The Tsimshian phrase for "There the fish jump!"

Button blanket: A robe of wool cloth, usually bright red in color, decorated on the back with a family crest outlined in tiny white buttons of mother-of-pearl.

Clan: A group of families with one common ancestor. The Tsimshian have four major clans: the Eagles, Wolves, Ravens, and Killer Whales.

Crest: An image of an animal adopted by a family or clan and used to decorate an object or article of clothing.

Frontlet: A carved wooden mask worn over the forehead as a part of a headdress, usually carved in the crest of the wearer.

Fry bread: Dough that has been deep-fried. Usually it is served with something sweet on top, such as maple syrup or honey. A favorite Tsimshian dessert.

Gikwah: *(geek-WAH)* The Tsimshian word meaning "Do it again!"

Hardtack: Bread made without yeast that looks like large, hard wafers. An important food to the early Tsimshian people, it could last for a long time without spoiling.

Klallam: *(KLAH-lum)* A coast Salish Indian tribe who live on a reservation called Little Boston, near Port Gamble, Washington.

Lap'aigh laskeeg: *(lah-pah-AG-a-lah-SKEEK)* The Tsimshian phrase for "He Who Flies Like the Eagle." It is David's Indian name.

Metlakatla: *(MET-lah-CAT-lah)* A settlement in southern Alaska on Annette Island where a large group of Tsimshian live.

Potlatch: A ceremony in which presents are given or exchanged. The potlatch was the high point of the Tsimshians' social life. The person who could give away the most gifts, especially valuable ones, achieved the highest status.

Puget Sound: A large body of water that separates the Olympic Peninsula from the rest of Washington state.

Regalia: The costumes worn by the Indian people during their ceremonies.

Reservation: Public land set aside for the use of Native American tribes.

Speaker stick: A long, straight pole that is carved with the crest of the chief and shows that he is the leader of the tribe. When the chief holds it, the people listen to his words of advice or wisdom.

Spirit Helper: A figure or animal carved on a hook to attract fish or show ownership.

Totem: An animal or object from which a family traces its clan origins.

Totem pole: A tall pole carved from a single log with a design showing several totems stacked one upon the other. Totem poles are made to honor an individual or to tell a legend or story.

Trade cloth: A strong woolen cloth woven by the Europeans who brought it to the northwest to trade for furs and other goods. The cloth was used by the Indians to make blankets and robes.

Tradition: The handing down of customs or beliefs from one generation to another.

Tribe: A group of persons or clans with one common language and living under a leader or chief.

Trickster: A character or person who delights in playing tricks on others and is skilled at doing so. In the Tsimshian stories, Raven was a well-known trickster.

Tsimshian: *(TSIM-shee-an)* A tribe of Northwest Coast Indians who came from the banks of the Nass and Skeena Rivers of British Columbia.

INDEX

Numbers in *italics* refer to pages with photos